This book is published strictly for historical purposes.
The Naval and Military Press Ltd
expressly bears no responsibility or liability of any type,
to any first, second or third party, for any harm,
injury or loss whatsoever.

THE ART OF IN-FIGHTING

Fig. 1—The Author in Private Life.

THE ART OF IN-FIGHTING

A TREATISE ON A TOO NEGLECTED SCIENCE

BY
FRANK KLAUS

EX-MIDDLE-WEIGHT CHAMPION OF THE WORLD

The Naval & Military Press Ltd

Published by

The Naval & Military Press Ltd
Unit 5 Riverside, Brambleside
Bellbrook Industrial Estate
Uckfield, East Sussex
TN22 1QQ England

Tel: +44 (0)1825 749494

www.naval-military-press.com
www.nmarchive.com

*In reprinting in facsimile from the original, any imperfections are inevitably reproduced
and the quality may fall short of modern type and cartographic standards.*

CONTENTS.

	PAGE
INTRODUCTION—WHAT IS IN-FIGHTING?	13—24
GETTING IN TO CLOSE QUARTERS	26
STOPPING LEFT LEAD AND GETTING IN TO PUNCH THE RIBS	30
SIDE-STEPPING LEFT, AND GETTING HOME WITH LEFT ON THE HEART	31
GUARDING AGAINST DANGER WHEN ATTACKING—LEFT JOLT TO PLACE THE DEADLY RIGHT	32
IN-FIGHTER'S MOST DEADLY PUNCH	34
AVOIDING A DRIVING RIGHT, BLOCKING THE LEFT, AND PUNCHING STOMACH	35
FORCING AN OPPONENT TO THE ROPES	36
THE LIVER PUNCH	38
WATCHING AN OPPONENT'S LEGS WHEN HUGGING	40
FEIGNING "GROGGINESS"	44
THE EYES AND THE BRAIN	44
RIGHT HOOK TO THE JAW—A REMEDY FOR THE PUSHING BOXER	48
WHEN A PUNCH LOOKS EASY	50
PRECONCEIVED ATTACKS	50
RECONNOITRING WHEN AT CLOSE QUARTERS	54

	PAGE
PLACING THE RIGHT-ARM JOLT	54
THE JAB	56
BEATING AN OPPONENT BY PUNCHING HIS GLOVED HANDS OR ARMS	58
BREAKING APART AN OPPONENT'S ARMS TO FACILITATE AN ATTACK	64
IN-FIGHTING PHASES IN ACTUAL CONTESTS	64
PUNCHING THE OPPONENT WHO HOLDS	65
WHEN TO HOLD AN OPPONENT	66
HOOKING THE RIGHT WHILE THE LEFT IS BEING HELD	66
BREAKING AWAY SAFELY	70
HOLDING AN ARM IN CHANCERY	72
TRAINING	73

ILLUSTRATIONS.

THE AUTHOR IN PRIVATE LIFE . . FRONTISPIECE	
	PAGE
FRANK KLAUS, EX-MIDDLE-WEIGHT CHAMPION OF THE WORLD	15
FRANK KLAUS AND HIS SPARRING PARTNER, FRANK MADOLE	17
AN OBVIOUS OPENING FOR THE IN-FIGHTER .	19
PUSHING THE LEFT LEAD ASIDE, AND GETTING IN ON THE RIBS, LIVER OR HEART . .	21
A DEVASTATING PUNCH TO THE HEART, FOLLOWED BY RIGHT TO THE RIBS . . .	23
THE IN-FIGHTER'S MOST DEADLY PUNCH: THE RIGHT DRIVE TO THE PIT OF THE STOMACH	25
A SMART TRIPLE MOVEMENT: SIDE-STEPPING RIGHT, STOPPING LEFT, AND GETTING HOME ON STOMACH	27
RUSHING AN OPPONENT TO THE ROPES . .	29
THE LIVER PUNCH, AFTER CATCHING OPPONENT'S RIGHT ON THE NECK	33
WATCHING YOUR OPPONENT'S LEG MOVEMENTS	37
THE RIGHT UPPER-CUT TO THE JAW, AFTER DUCKING YOUR OPPONENT'S RIGHT . .	39

	PAGE
THE RIGHT HOOK TO THE JAW.	41
THE PUNCH TO THE HEART. THE RESULT OF A PRECONCEIVED DELIVERY	43
LOOKING UP FOR AN OPENING TO THE JAW	45
GETTING HOME WITH THE RIGHT-ARM JOLT	47
PARALYSING AN OPPONENT'S ARM BY PUNCHING HIS BICEPS	49
MAKING AN OPENING BY BREAKING OPPONENT'S ARMS APART	51
USING LEFT ON THE OPPONENT WHO HOLDS	53
BRINGING ABOUT A DOUBLE CLINCH FOR THE REFEREE'S INTERVENTION	55
HOOKING THE MAN WHO HOLDS	57
HOOKING RIGHT ON FINDING THE LEFT STOPPED	59
THE SAFE "BREAK".	61
THE LEFT ARM IN CHANCERY	63
PUNCHING BODY WITH THE RIGHT, WHILE LEFT IS BEING HELD	67
A PECULIAR INCIDENT: PAPKE FALLING ON TO A PUNCH	69
GEORGE ENGEL, MANAGER TO FRANK KLAUS	71

PREFACE.

In writing this book I hope to supply a want.

By that I mean the bringing to light of a far too little known science, which seems to have been but elementarily studied by the modern-day boxer.

And how all-important! How many pugilistic battles have been lost owing to an altogether inadequate knowledge of the most vital principle of boxing! The old-fashioned hit, stop and get-away system, although still the predominant note in the noble art, has been sensibly strengthened, yet it is remarkable to realise how few boxers are aware of this fact.

Without wishing to claim any particular beauty for in-fighting, years of practical experience have convinced me that it is, perhaps, the most effective weapon in the hands of the boxer to-day. Conservatism is as fatal to boxing as it is when applied to any other form of sport.

I am sorry to say that in England this sentiment, as applied to the art of boxing and contemporary pastimes, is rampant. The last Olympic Games were a potential testimony to this particular state of things.

In France there appears to exist a greater tendency to "move with the times." Such boxers as Georges Carpentier succeed where others fail, owing to this desire to delve into the "up to date" in things athletic.

Without being of very recent origin, in-fighting has never been practised with such devastating effects as at the present day.

The all-dominating feature of a contest surely lies in the beating of an opponent. How can this be done with any degree of confidence, if one enters upon a battle inadequately armed ?

Taking all other things as equal, such as weight, endurance, training and skill, the man with the better idea of in-fighting must " come out on top.

This is but a logical deduction, one that should appeal to the young boxer just launching on a pugilistic career. Such defeats as those sustained by Bombardier Billy Wells are generally the result of an incomplete fistic education, that is to say, of a lack of in-fighting experience. The old notion that the straight left will beat any man is distinctly out of gear in these times, especially when we have such examples as those afforded us by Palzer and Gunboat Smith when they defeated the Bombardier.

Victory in each of these instances appears to have favoured the man who knew just the moment to get to close quarters, and annul all the work done by the more stylish boxer. If, as must be generally admitted, only victory counts in a boxing contest, then it is for us to find the best means to secure this desirable end.

From a spectacular point of view, in-fighting seems to lose in comparison with the stand-up long-range methods. This brings me to the point as to whether it is better to be what is known as a " pretty boxer " and remain a mediocrity or study further and more effectual principles and thus become a champion.

In-fighting is very like an olive; one wants educating up to its taste, so to speak. The reason that close-range boxing is not popular must be that it is not understood. To dislike a thing is to condemn it, in spite of its intrinsic merits.

There is really just as much beauty in in-fighting as there is in all the more familiar phases of the noble art; the fault mostly lies in the fact that the public refuse to see it.

It is my earnest desire to delineate in this little volume not only the hidden secrets and artistic merits of in-fighting, but to show its imperative utility to all.

Having perused, studied, inwardly digested and thoroughly mastered its subtleties, I trust that readers may have found a new force in its relation to the noble art of self-defence.

I should also like to take this opportunity of thanking my excellent manager, George Engel, my sparring partner, Frank Madole, and my friend, F. H. Hurdman Lucas (of "Boxing"), for the valuable assistance they have given me in producing this little work.

THE AUTHOR.

INTRODUCTION.

What is In-Fighting?

To this question I might easily reply, that in-fighting is out-fighting's greatest ally. The one can strike more effectually with the help of the other, and yet it is a remarkable fact that but few boxers realise this truism.

Two forces are always better than one. Although the knock-out frequently occurs as the result of a long-range punch, a boxer is necessarily heavily handicapped when opposed to another who is equally capable of inflicting decisive defeat at close quarters.

The inference here is obvious : arm yourself with every available means of victory, thus reducing the elements of bad luck to a minimum, and by that I mean that a boxer equipped with all the necessary knowledge of in-fighting and its attendant forces reduces his chances of defeat.

How often do we hear of the " lucky punch being responsible for a boxer's defeat ! Without for a moment wishing to deny that the element of luck plays some part in boxing contests, victory is generally acquired by the more skilful ; by the boxer who, possessed of a more profound knowledge of the game, imposes it on an opponent.

To sum up, in-fighting is an all too-neglected art, one that at any moment during a contest is capable of turning defeat into victory. It is the artillery of pugilism ; the besieging force that, by its continual pounding at the outer walls of an opposing element, finally reduces it to capitulation. Of course, strategy must play an important part in this particular form of boxing, as it must in every other.

Strategy: Good and Bad.

How often has superior strategy won the day when applied even to superior forces ?

This very important part of a boxer's in-fighting education cannot be imparted   it should develop with experience.

Seldom is it that two boxers follow exactly the same style. It therefore remains for the one or the other to formulate his plan of attack and defence according to the particular idiosyncrasies of his opponent.

Some there are whose peculiarity is to protect the jaw with an almost motherly care.

This very action is an indication of weakness on that man's part, his protective spirit but acting as a clue for the locating of the vulnerable spot in his composition.

Others will at once expose their weakest part by the slightest gesture. A feint at the stomnach, for instance, will sometimes make an opponent gasp in expectation of the punch that he thinks is coming.

Fig. 2—Frank Klaus, Ex-Middle-Weight Champion of the World.

Such a one should prove an easy prey for the in-fighter, for by judicious manœuvring it is possible to so demoralise the boxer with the frail body as to finally beat him.

The strategy of making an opponent either drop or bring his hands up, therby compelling him to expose a vital spot, is as old as the hills as regards long-range boxing. Successive feints will often accomplish the purpose, but with in-fighting the modus operandi is totally different.

Feinting while at Close Quarters.

Whereas ordinary feinting is but the implied delivery of a punch, meant to disconcert an opponent or put him off his guard, for the purpose of finding the necessary opening for a preconceived delivery, no such strategy is possible in in-fighting.

When close up to an opponent, punching becomes a matter of intuition. One can neither properly see what an opponent is going to do, nor is it often possible to be guided by our eyesight as to the most exposed or attackable parts of his body.

At close range boxing becomes instinctive, that is, we must rely mostly upon the sense of touch to know exactly where and when to place a punch.

This particular development of the in-fighting art may be acquired through following the instructions given in this volume, and practising them often with as many sparring partners as it is possible to find.

To always box with the same man is but to fall into a single groove, from which it is extremely difficult to extricate oneself. Although there are

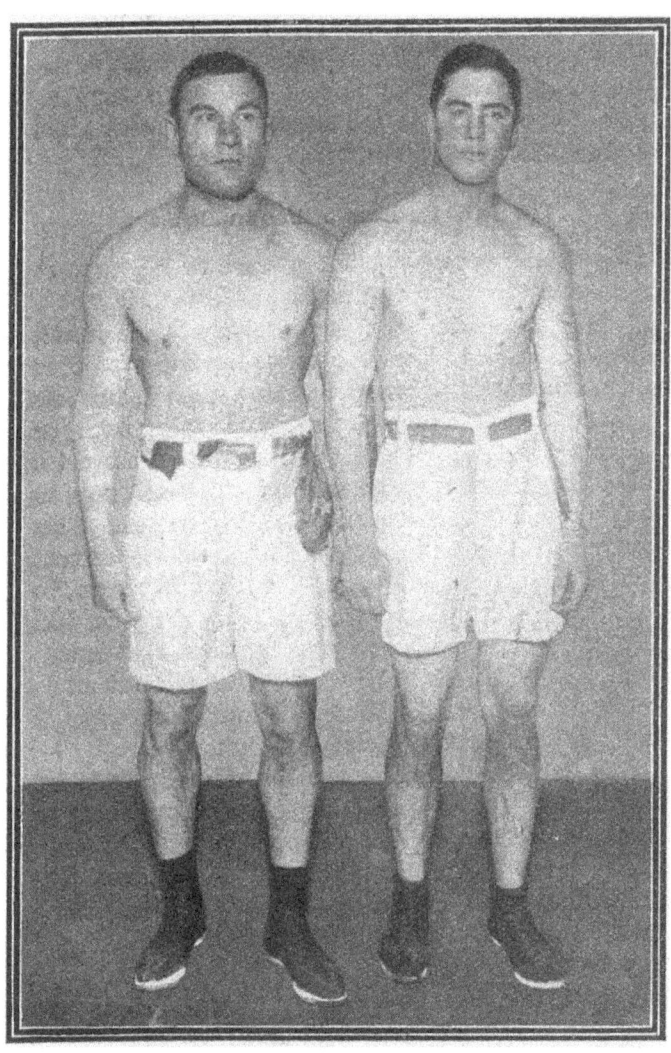

Fig. 3—Frank Klaus and his Sparring Partner, Frank Madole.

but few variants of the straight left and right cross-counter, in-fighting offers new fields for the exploiting of, and coming into contact with, unsuspected elements of the pugilistic art.

The Infinite Possibilites in Boxing.

Although apparently simple, and to all appearances composed of but a few essentialities, the noble art, like the violin, is never thoroughly mastered, This assertion may seem strange to those who in boxing see but the giving of a blow with either left or right fist, the blocking of same, stepping back, or ducking. But like the instrument just referred to, and although with practically but as few strings to work upon, boxing is ever full of variations. This theory is based on the possibility of the almost infinite transposal of, say, the numbers one to twenty. As is well known, these may be placed in thousands of ways, each one showing a different total. So is it with boxing, for, although but made up of an apparently limited gamut, its range of possibilities is well-nigh without end.

This is especially noticeable with in-fighting, wherein one must not only depend upon punching an opponent, but so negative his counter attacks as to always have the better of him. In-fighting (the same rule applies to boxing generally) is not wholly the inflicting of punishment, but the neutralising of an adversary's efforts.

A good defence is as necessary as a perfect attack, and although some men can take more punishment than others, a boxer has often but himself to blame

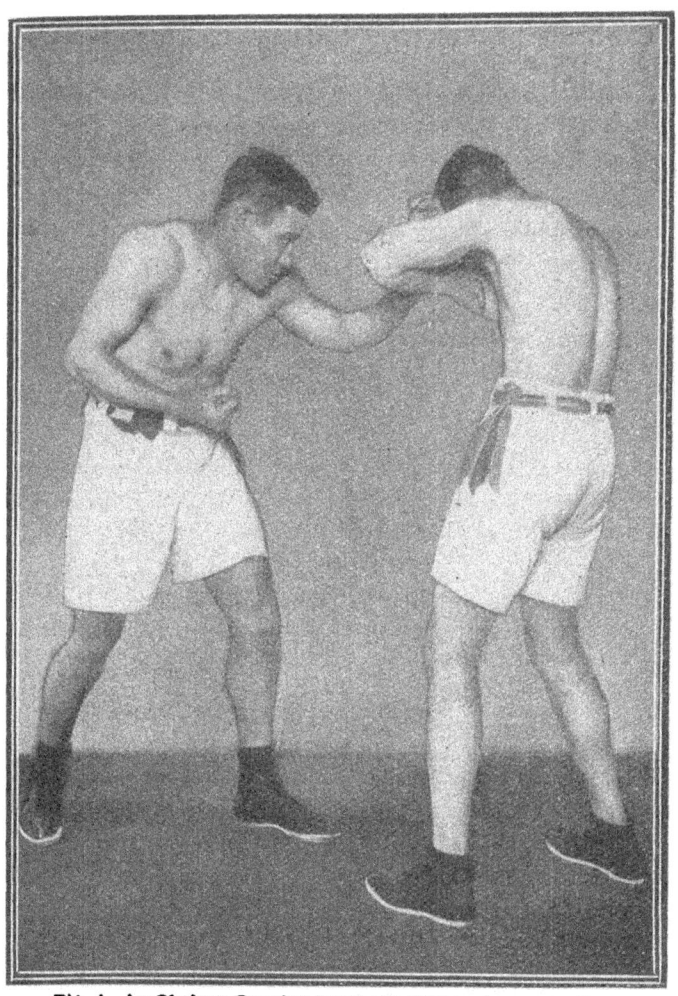

Fig. 4—An Obvious Opening for the In-Fighter (see page 28).

for boxing without the slightest regard for his individual qualities.

A good in-fighter, for instance, would be courting disaster in seeking to beat an opponent by long-range punching and vice versa. Boxers are often led to such imprudences either by losing their temper or being led into them by their opponent's wiles.

Generalship in In-Fighting.

This brings us to ringcraft or generalship. As I said, feinting, as generally understood, is next to impossible in close quarters; for the simple reason that the two boxers depend entirely upon the sense of touch. Instead of feinting, therefore, it would perhaps be better to substitute the word cunning or craft, when applied to in-fighting, or, better still, generalship. The aim of a general, we all know, is to deceive the enemy, but whereas there are many ways of doing this at long-range boxing, the field for such strategy is narrowed up while in-fighting.

The Waiting Game.

If, by his style of boxing, your opponent should have practically intimated the fact that he has a weak stomach, it is bad generalship to immediately attack that particular spot. Let the in-fighter direct his attention to the ribs and liver, with an occasional visit "higher up." The chances are that he will sooner or later find the opening that he has patiently waited for. The same strategy applies to the jaw. A boxer with a "glass" chin invariably

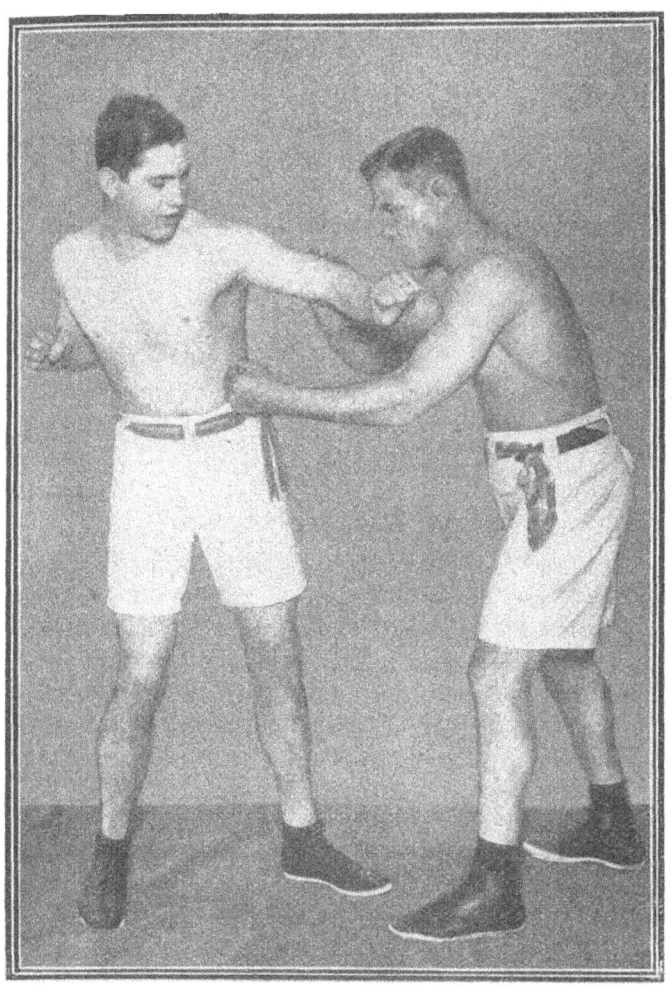

Fig. 5—Pushing the Left Lead aside, and getting in on the Ribs, Liver or Heart.

believes himself safe when at close quarters, and, although perhaps an indifferent in-fighter, he will seek that which he fondly believes should prove immunity from danger, in continual hugs.

Although it will be next to impossible to reach that man's jaw at such times, it remains for the in-fighter to so weaken his opponent by body punches as to eventually find little or no difficulty in catching him on the vulnerable " point " after the break.

The in-fighter's most deadly work is effected on the body (see Fig. 10, p. 33), although the jolt (Fig. 16, p. 47) and half-arm hooks (see Fig. 13, p. 41) to the chin, eyes, nose, and mouth play no small part in helping an opponent to eventual defeat.

Acquiring the Intuitive Instinct.

Generalship (or craft) in in-fighting is mostly a gift. It is the intuitive appreciation of things at the psychological moment, the knowing by his smallest and apparently insignificant gesture or movement what an opponent is about to do. This gift may be sensibly developed by the observant boxer if he will follow my previous counsel, and find as many sparring partners as he can with varying styles.

Having done this and furthermore, conscientiously practised all the moves set forth in this volume, there is every reason to hope that the subject, be he professional or amateur, will have armed himself with yet one more essentiality for his complete pugilistic education—as complete as such a curriculum can be, for in boxing there seems to be always something new to learn.

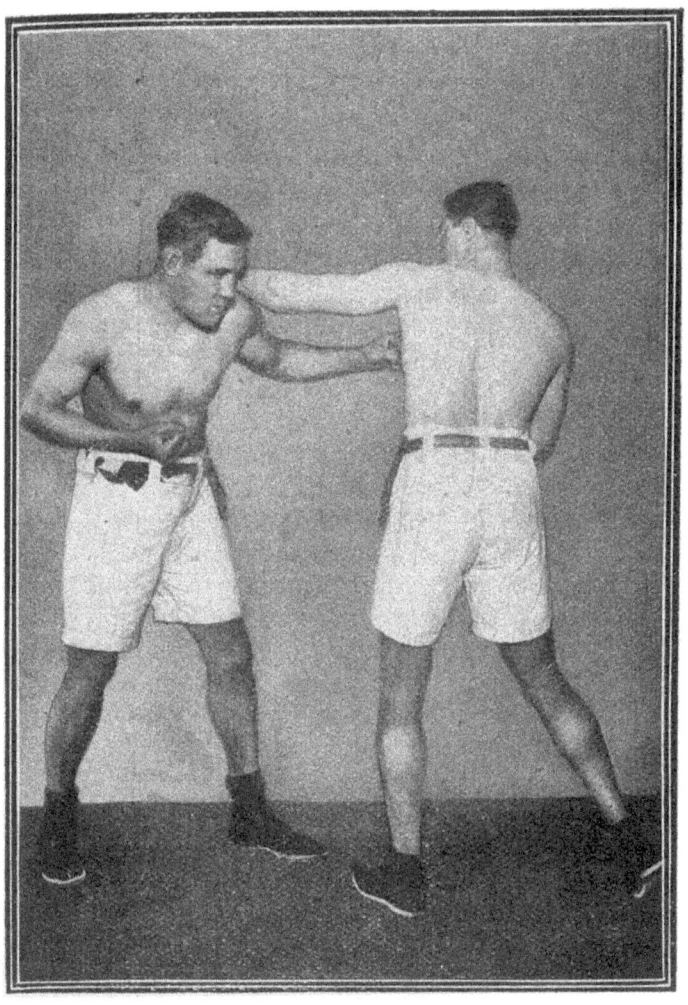

Fig. 6—A Devastating Punch to the Heart, Followed by the Right to the Ribs.

Conclusion.

In-fighting is one of these new things, for in recommending it to my readers it is with the belief and hope that they are already proficient in the art of long-range boxing.

As I said at the commencement of this little work, the one cannot be complete without the other, whereas the two must perforce make for a perfect whole.

Although I have made a special study of in-fighting and gained most of my contests by its aid, out-fighting has been an equally important factor in my successes. Many books have been writen on boxing generally, but the art of in-fighting has always played a very subordinate part therein.

Seeing the really great importance of this all too-neglected department of the noble art, the idea occurred to me to specialise it in this book. I trust that it may be the means of turning out more complete boxers than has hitherto been the case.

Fig. 7—The In-Fighter's most Deadly Punch: the Right Drive to the pit of the Stomach.

THE MOST IMPORTANT IN-FIGHTING PHASES DESCRIBED AND ILLUSTRATED.

Getting in to Close Quarters.

Never be careless, even while practising. There is a psychological moment for all things in this life, but none is so important as to know the right one to get to close quarters with an opponent. This again, I might say, is mostly a matter of intuitive appreciation, for all movements in boxing are but momentary. To let the proper chance slip by is, perhaps, to lose a contest. By practice the eye becomes easily trained to this sort of telepathic communication from an opponent. Some boxers do not worry at all about anything when in the " gym " save the ordinary rudiments of boxing. They are pleased to just punch a sparring partner all the while. Knowing perfectly well that there is but little danger of being damaged themselves, this breeds acute carelessness that deteriorates a man's science and lessens his mental vitality. A boxer should be just as alert in the " gym " as he is in a ring, and always on the qui vive for new things, of which the game is full.

Thus it is that the choosing of just the right time to bore in to an opponent for in-fighting purposes is mostly a matter of acuteness of minute observation. In spite of that, there are moments when such openings are so obvious that a good in-fighter instantly sees the opportunity for the carrying out of his

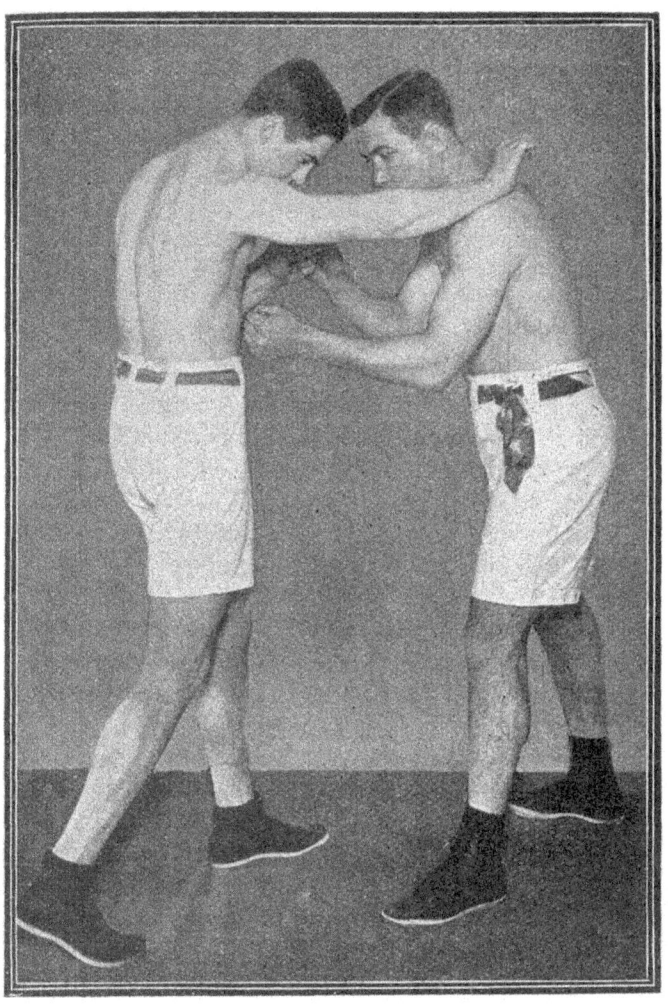

Fig. 8—A Smart Triple Movement: Side-stepping Right, Stopping Left, and getting home on Stomach.

deadly work (see Fig. 4, p. 19). In this instance it will be observed that the opponent is backing away from a punch that has apparently stung him, the while he subconsciously covers his jaw.

A man on the retreat becomes the prey of the in-fighter, for to recover his backward impetus he must perforce come to a standstill before resuming any forward tendency. That is the time to rush him (before he can recover an aggressive advance), force him to the ropes (see Fig. 9, p. 29), and there have things all one's own way.

A man leaning with his back to the ropes is at the greatest disadvantage possible, for apart from the natural anxiety of finding himself so penned in, he can but use his defensive qualities to extricate himself from so perilous a position. I worked this out with much success during my contest with Papke, for most of the time I had him pinned on the cords practically helpless (see Fig. 23, p. 61). This was my plan of campaign, for being himself a wonderful in-fighter, I had to use this stratagem to out-general his generalship.

Opposed to a good out-fighter, so much "rope-fighting" is not necessary, for the while he is sending out straight lefts and long-range rights, the opportunities for closing in are manifold.

The most difficult man for the in-fighter to deal with is he whose footwork keeps him constantly on the move. Such a boxer wants watching as a cat watches a mouse, for, unless the in-fighter be very sure of his attack, a fast-footed opponent will often side-step a rush and make the former look foolish.

Fig. 9—Rushing an Opponent to the Ropes.

Too much of this is necessarily detrimental, not only to the in-fighter's stamina, but also from the fact that it influences the referee or judges to be highly impressed with his adversary's cleverness.

In-fighting and footwork are alienated. This is obvious, seeing that the most effectual work of the in-fighter's is accomplished when mobility is impossible. Therefore, I repeat, to continually seek close fighting with such an opponent is but to create an unfavourable impression. Therefore, when meeting a "ring scorcher," let him come to you. He must clinch at some time or another, then bring your in-fighting batteries into action. That he may not be able to break away before you have punished him some, it is advisable, the while you are doing this, to bring all the necessary "pushing" power into your blows, and thus force your man to the ropes. Once there, the punching should become crisp and sharp.

Checking the Boxer with a Good Left.

Stopping Left Lead and getting in to Punch the Ribs.

A boxer with a good left will naturally make ample use of that particular member during the whole of a contest. It therefore wants watching and stopping. The out-fighter will invariably block the punch with his right, cross-counter it with right to the jaw, or counter with left. While sometimes carrying out these excellent maxims, the in-fighter has yet other means by which he may not only effectually nullify the left lead, but thus make an opening for close-range punches to the ribs, liver and heart. Of course, it may not succeed every time, but the devastation wrought on an opponent's body during these periodical attacks soon begins to tell its tale. As will be seen in the illustration (Fig. 5, p. 21), the getting outside of a left lead, and pushing same aside with the right, tends to over-balance the opponent and nullify his possible punch with the right. This leaves the body exposed for the in-fighter's left on any vulnerable part of the body.

This particular movement requires a deal of practice, the necessary assurance being acquired only after long acquaintance with its intricacies. It looks simple, but as the parry must be effected as shown, namely, above the opponent's elbow, I should advise plenty of trials in the " gym " before trying it in a ring. It will then become almost an instinct, but as I said above, this particular move must be varied with the out-fighting method of counteracting the left lead to face. It is always bad policy to keep on doing the same thing during a contest. The better boxer is often he, who, by his craft, baffles his opponent all through a bout.

Side-stepping Left, and getting Home with Left on the Heart.

This movement resembles the last in many respects, but instead of pushing aside the left as before, the in-fighter must side-step it, thus leaving the opponent's heart exposed for a left hook. Having delivered this punch, the right is able to follow up with a " dig " to the ribs.

As will be seen, it is almost impossible for an opponent to retaliate in time, for his own left acts as a guard for one's head, thus rendering his right harmless. His only hope in such a case is to clinch, but as the two before-mentioned punches have presumably done some damage, this getting to close quarters by the opponent is but playing into the in-fighter's hands. Should the former see fit to step back instead of clinching, that is the moment to force close quarters by rushing him to the ropes and there continuing the body work until the referee breaks. As will be seen from the illustration, a certain amount of risk must be taken in getting one's head outside the left lead, but having successfully accomplished the side-stepping movement, all is plain sailing. It is here necessary for me to explain that, next to the punch to the pit of the stomach, a blow under or near the heart is perhaps the most devastating anywhere on the body. In either instance the man so punished is liable to take an excursion to the boards for any count, up to the "out."

Guarding against Danger when Attacking.
A Left Jolt to Place the Deadly Right.

This is one of the most important factors in in-fighting, as it is, by the way, at long-range work. In the former case, however, its virtues are all the more salient, seeing that the in-fighter, if not very skilled, courts a deal of danger. It is therefore incumbent upon him, when about to get to close quarters, to think as much of the possibilities of **receiving a nasty blow as of giving same.**

Fig. 10—The Liver Punch, after catching Opponent's Right on the Neck.

Some boxers there are who will attack an opponent with but one set object, namely, to deliver a certain fancied punch. Irrespective of a possibly dangerous counter attack, these men will wade into an opponent for the sole purpose of accomplishing that which is in their mind.

The in-fighter's thoughts should rest on the two possibilities, and thus proceed on the necessary caution and generalship. As will be seen in Fig. 7' my object was to get the right home to the pit of the stomach.

The In-Fighter's most Deadly Punch.

This is undoubtedly the most deadly in-fighting punch possible, and means decisive victory if properly administered. In trying for this, however, it must be remembered that a right may come along and upset our plan. Therefore the left is brought up to the opponent's chin almost simultaneously with the right drive to the mark. If successful the left jolt should send your man's head back, a movement which causes the muscles of his stomach to relax. As will be seen in the illustration, the in-fighter leaves his face open somewhat for his opponent's left. But admitting that the former has not been successful with the said attack, the left may be quickly brought round to cover or the head lowered into the right shoulder, thus protecting the jaw. This last movement would naturally cause the opponent's left to land on the head and not the chin.

Avoiding a Driving Right, Blocking the Left, and Punching Stomach.

The opponent in this picture has lashed out with the right, but the quick-witted in-fighter's move is to at once wade into his man and make the punch non-effectual, that is, presuming the said right hand punch has been a straight drive to the chin, not a hook or swing. The dodging of this delivery, by quickly stepping in with the head slightly on one side, has the effect of carrying your opponent's right clean out of its straight course, so to speak, and making it shoot over the shoulder. The impetus created by the sending forth of the said punch, and the missing of same, is such that you are well into close quarters before your man can regain his proper striking equilibrium. Seeing himself thus forcibly brought into close contact with the in-fighter, the opponent will try to do a bit of short-range work himself, and his right arm being momentarily out of action, the possibilities are that he will attempt a half-arm left hook to your now exposed chin. You must watch this, and catch the punch in the palm of your right hand, at the same time driving the left to the stomach. The result of this will invariably be to compel your opponent to bring his right back to protect the body, in which case the in-fighter's left must get outside it in an upward hook to the chin. This may lead to an exchange at close quarters, during which the experienced in-fighter should again have things a good deal his own way. Of course, there is no knowing exactly what an opponent will do; but as I have written elsewhere, the thorough digesting of this work, followed by plenty of practice, should breed the in-fighting instinct in most of my readers enthusiastically bent upon acquiring same.

Forcing an Opponent to the Ropes.

As I have said elsewhere, the most deadly in-fighting is served out to an opponent when he is on the ropes. The point, therefore, is to get him there as often as possible. Rugged boxers want a deal of hustling, while those who depend mostly on mobility, or fast footwork, are difficult to catch. But even these must at some time or another find themselves off their balance, or should I say that it should be the in-fighter's object to effect this unsteadiness of foot ? The hit, stand, and get-away boxer may never bring about this desirable state of affairs himself, for having scored with a punch, he usually skips back to contemplate the effect of his shot. This allows the opponent to regain any slight overbalancing that the blow may have caused.

The in-fighter, on the contrary, must at once follow up a hard punch, and by so doing create a further unsteadiness in his opponent's equipoise. That is the moment to rush him, thus compelling the retreating boxer to lose his left foothold and fall back on the right. In the illustration, Fig. 9, Madole's full weight at that moment is on one leg, so that he is forced to step back to avoid falling altogether. The in-fighter must not relax his forward movement until he has his man well up against the ropes. The impact thus created will force most

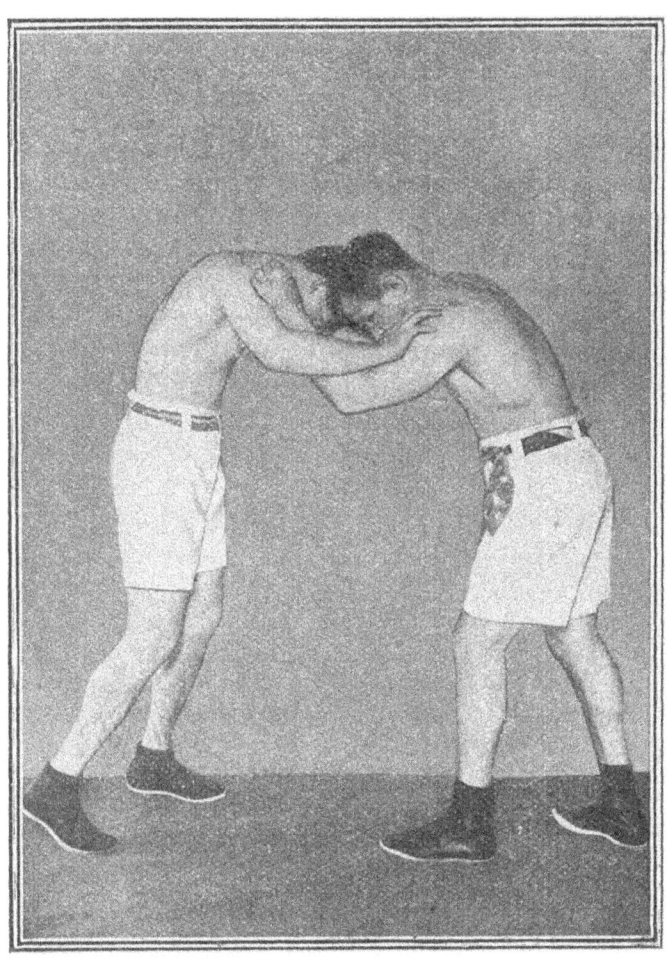

Fig. 11—Watching your Opponent's Leg Movements.

boxers to bend their backs over the top cord, this movement causing them to leave their stomachs open for the in-fighter's demolishing work.

As in all other moves of the boxing game, the in-fighter must choose the psychological moment to rush his opponent. If this does not present itself, then he must use all his in-fighting strategy to make it. For it must be remembered that one of the greatest arts in boxing is creating favourable opportunities for oneself; that is to say, using every honest means to compel an opponent to do just the very thing that he himself would avoid. That is where generalship comes in, that ever necessary element in all engagements wherein the "fortunes of war" play an important part.

The Liver Punch.

After the stomach and heart, the liver is the most vulnerable part of a boxer's body, that is, now that the kidney punch has been barred. This measure meant the taking away of a valuable point of vantage for the in-fighter, inasmuch as the kidneys were the easiest part of a man to punch, while incurring the minimum of risk. Nevertheless, it is perhaps as well for the boxing game, and boxers generally, that these delicate regions were ruled out and declared forbidden ground. This action was extremely unfavourable to the close range expert, but it was necessary, if only from the fact of the deterioration of a boxer's health after having been severely mauled by the kidney fiend. Personally I never made much use of the punch so that its exclusion was but a small loss to me.

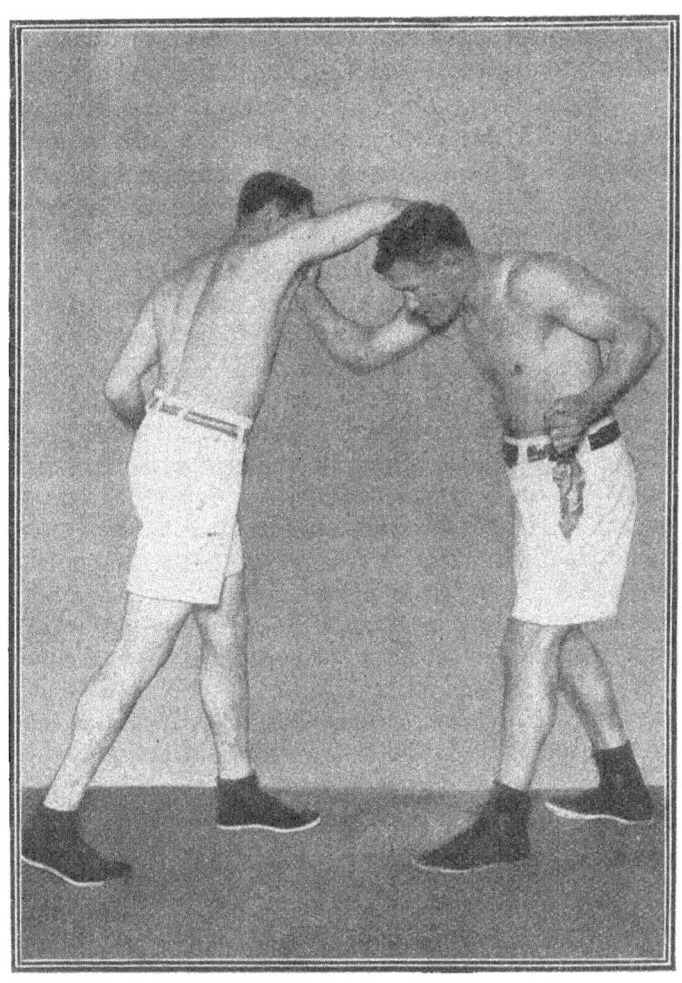

Fig. 12—The Right Upper-Cut to the Jaw, after Ducking your Opponent's Right.

In its place I made a study of the liver punch, which, although less painful, plays no small part in an opponent's undoing. As with all in-fighting punches, it is best delivered when your man is on the ropes, but that does not necessarily imply that it cannot be tried at any other moment, and failing being able to reach his man, the in-fighter must await a right swing, or hook, from his opponent, catch same on the neck, and close in. When doing this, always keep your eye on the left that may come up unpleasantly near your chin. The right should be ready to stop this, while your left is driven to the liver. The blow is clearly illustrated in Fig. 10 (p. 33), and with a little practice should add yet one more weapon to a boxer's arsenal. Should the opponent's left be slow in coming, then there is a splendid opportunity to smash your right home to his spleen, and thus complete the full object of your incursion to close quarters. Few boxers can take many punches on the liver or spleen without weakening. Fitzsimmons knew this, and made an art of this particular blow, as well as the shift-punch to the stomach. As he was perhaps the greatest middle-weight who ever lived, these specialities of his need no further recommendation.

Watch an Opponent's Legs, Knees, and Feet when Hugging.

As it is mostly impossible, when at close quarters, to watch an opponent's eyes (it being advisable to keep the head down), my advice is, watch his feet. These are often indicative of a boxer's intention, for

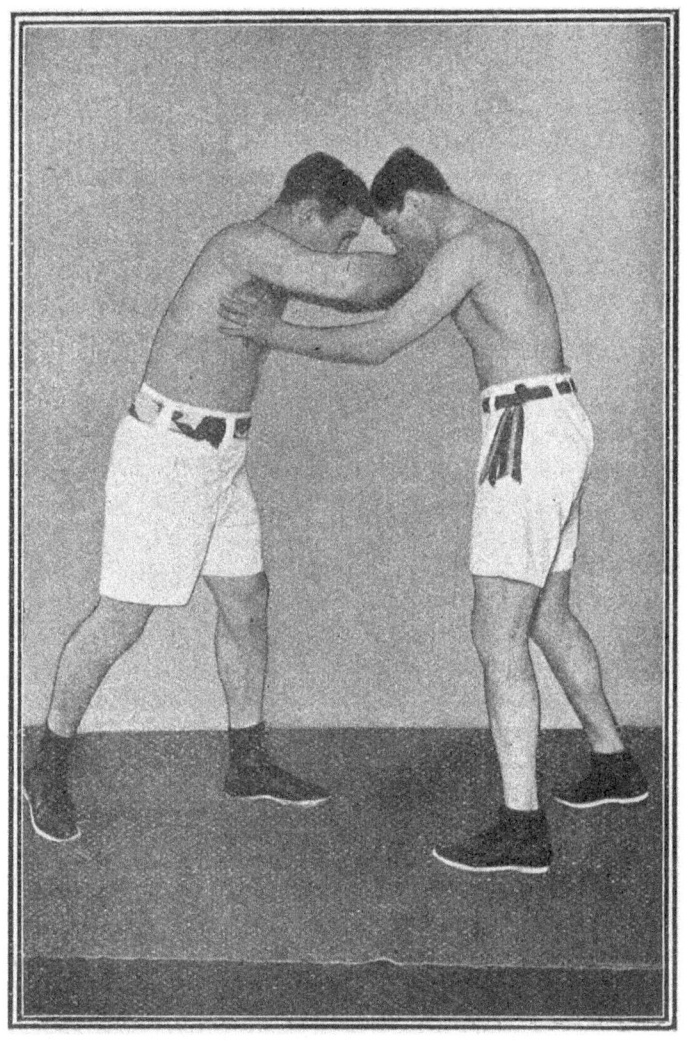

Fig. 13—The Right Hook to the Jaw.

the least forward movement means that he is himself trying to get closer in for short-range work. If, on the contrary, his feet show a tendancy to retreat, then you may rest assured that your opponent does not fancy close exchanges. Should the position, as shown in Fig. 11 (p. 37), be unfavourable to effectual body pasting, then the in-fighter may either allow his man to step away, or do so himself, in the hope of securing a more suitable opening for his particular talents.

Apart from that, it is always interesting to know the exact effect of a punch on an opponent, and this is possible by a glance at his legs and knees.

These parts seem to be in strange sympathy with the upper part of a man's body, and will at once by their firmness, or relaxation, communicate to the experienced eye the amount of damage done by a blow. Thus it is that we hear of a boxer "going groggy at the knees," or that his "legs shook" after a certain punch. If such an effect is produced by a long-range delivery it is obvious to the giver, for the receiver of the punch will insensibly "give himself away."

But in the case of a "knee-bending" punch at close quarters, what indication can the in-fighter have that the blow has been effectual, save by a glance at his opponent's legs? The first symptoms will be, that a boxer so "plugged" brings his whole weight to bear on you. Having gleaned so much, and lowered yourself to allow the full weight of your opponent's body to fall on his legs, your suspicions will be either verified or negatived.

Fig. 14—**The Punch** to the Heart. The result of a Preconceived Delivery.

Feigning "Grogginess."

There are boxers who will bring their histrionic talents to bear on a contest and feign " grogginess," in the hope of drawing you into a trap. Now, although this is more successful when practised while out-fighting, such ruses are not infrequent at close quarters. In the case of an opponent showing signs of distress, either feigned or real, it is the in-fighter's duty to immediately break clear, quickly survey the situation, and either keep away or drive the final punches home at a long or short range, according to his judgment.

Ducking an Opponent's Right Swing, Stepping in with Right Upper-cut, and Driving Left to the Stomach.

The Eyes and the Brain.

This is an exceedingly pretty part of the in-fighting art ; one, however, that should be well mastered before taking its possible risks. As the head has to play the master part of ducking the right swing, a deal of practice is necessary to know exactly when and how far the move is practicable. As in all phases of the Noble Art, the eye must accustom itself to possibilities, just as the brain must respond at once to the visual appreciation of danger or of openings for attack. The eyes are the outposts of the mind, so to speak, the transmission of its observations being carried with momentary rapidity to the centre of action—or headquarters.

Quick-wittedness in boxing may be developed by concentration during one's boxing, that is, a boxer must not for a single instant during a contest let

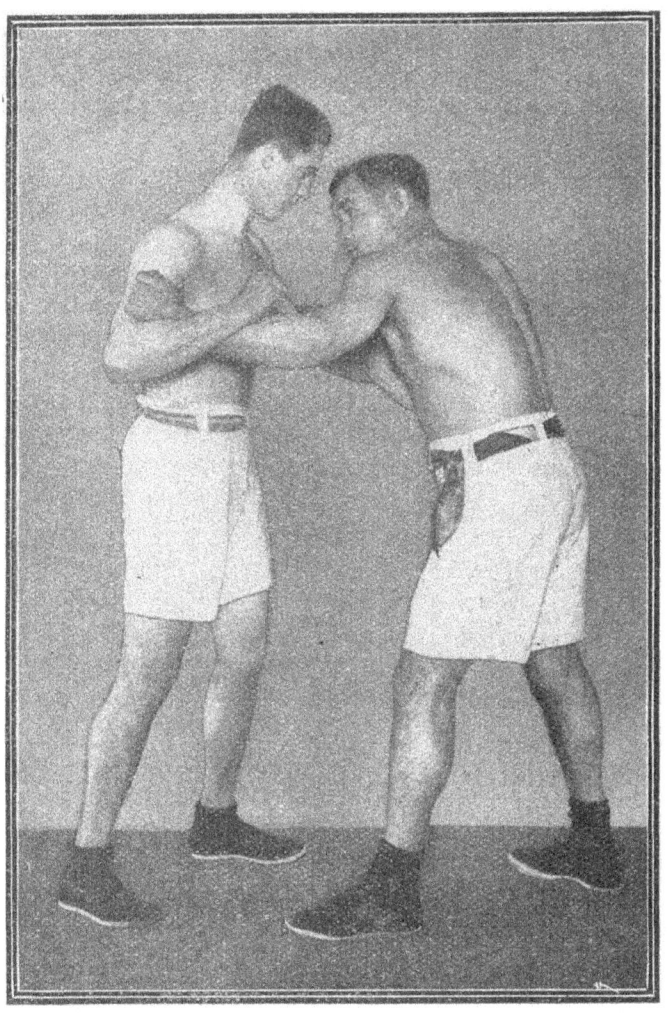

Fig. 15—Looking up for an Opening to the Jaw.

his imagination wander from his work. The same recommendation applies to the boxer when in the gymnasium, for the lack of interest in one's practice brings on laxity of mind at all times.

The beginner, especially, must realise that the boxing game is full of traps and surprises, that the eye must be trained to see these, and that the brain must work conjunctively in surmounting difficulties. It is necessary to impress these things firmly on the minds of those about to attempt the movement of Fig. 12. Having well reasoned out the possibilities of danger that an untimely or badly-executed lowering of the head may mean, let the reader practise it as often as possible, until the ducking becomes almost instinctive. Rome was not built in a day and it may take some time before this phase, as all others, by the way, is mastered sufficiently to be tried with safety during a real contest.

Once acquired, it is as simple as it is effectual, and means a big jump toward victory, if not the final step to that desirable end.

The missing of a right swing by an opponent usually means the slight losing of his equilibrium. This fact prevents him from bringing his left into motion in time to avoid the in-fighter's close-quarter upper-cut. Having ducked his right, the natural overbalancing of his body brings his chin into a direct upward line for the successful placing of your punch, as shown in the illustration. Before he can recover, the left may be easily driven to the stomach, the whole of which will lead to your man clinching, therefore the coming in for more short-range punish-

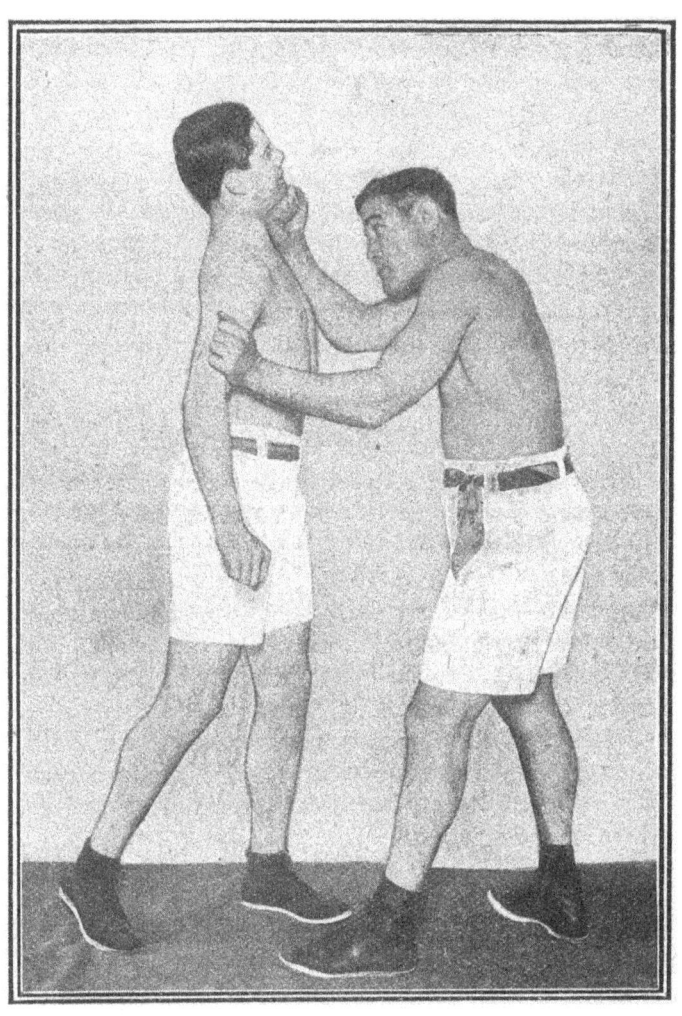

Fig. 16—Getting home with the Right Arm Jolt.

ment. As will be readily observed, the successful issue of all this depends entirely upon the proper ducking of your opponent's right swing at the psychological moment. The long-range boxer often ducks the same punch, but steps back in doing so. The in-fighter differs in that he must lower his head in a forward movement, thus preparing himself for the right upper-cut to the jaw and left body deliveries. A close study of the picture depicting this phase will convince anybody of its efficacy.

Right Hook to the Jaw.
A Remedy for the Pushing Boxer.

Although this punch may be given at all kinds of favourable moments, it should never be missed with the opponent who tries to push you away. The man who has suffered a good deal of body punishment from the in-fighter naturally does all he can to avoid the latter's continual " boring in," for, above all things, the close-range boxer must be on top of his man most of the time. The gamest of boxers get disheartened at these perpetual onslaughts, and seek every possible means of either keeping the in-fighter at a safe distance or of pushing him away when danger threatens.

Having, however, got to within easy striking distance, you will at times find your opponent making use of his hands to push you away. He is not holding, but just offering a desperate resistance to your advance. Dangerous as this proceeding is, numerous boxers will employ it in sheer desperation or pique. Of course, it is but asking for trouble,

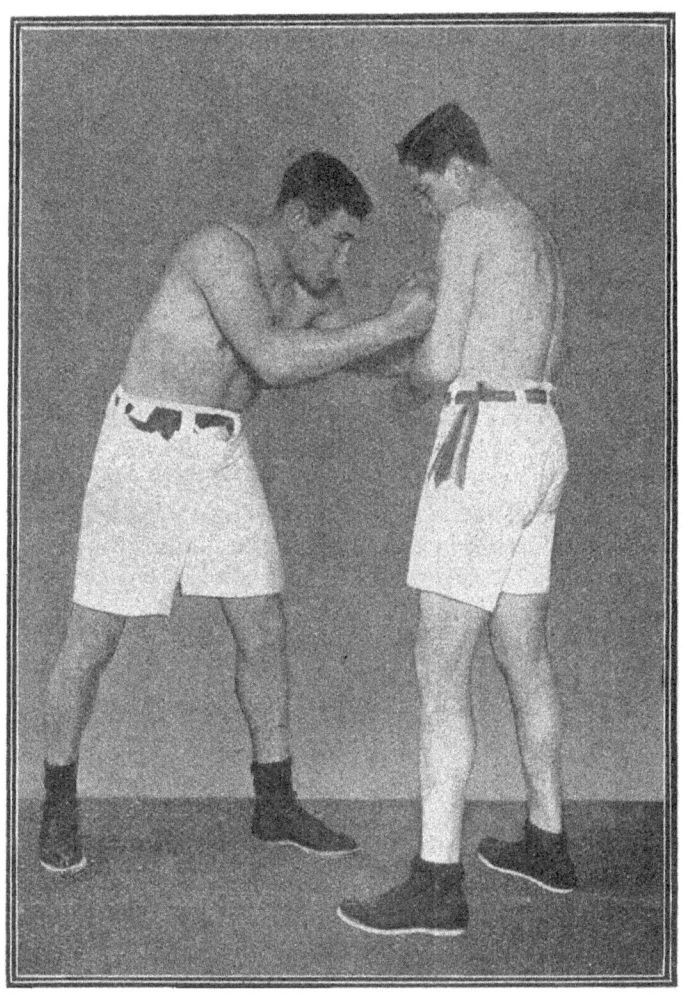

Fig. 17—Paralysing an Opponent's Arm by Punching his Biceps.

which should go out to them in the shape of a right half-arm hook to the jaw, the simplest shot in the world. This opportunity occurs but rarely, but if it does, as it must do in the course of a contest, then it is as well to be prepared for it, and not gasp at the simplicity of the punch.

When a Punch looks Easy.

"Asking" for a punch as it were is more often than not to avoid getting it, for it happens that the cutest of boxers will shy at the obviously easy punch, in the belief that it is but a trap. So few really easy things do occur during a battle, that perhaps boxers are wise in avoiding hidden pitfalls. In the case of the opponent who pushes you away, however, there is absolutely no reason why the right hook, as shown in the illustration, should not find a landing stage on that man's jaw.

Getting inside a Left Lead, Stopping the Right, and getting home on the Heart.
Preconceived Attacks.

As the left lead is the most conspicuous punch to deal with, the in-fighter must perforce use all his intelligence to counteract its numerous visitations. Blocking same with the right, ducking, stepping back, countering and crossing, are all possible replies, but the in-fighter has yet one more move in his curriculum. The feature of a punch should always be but the object of a preconceived force line; that is to say, that a blow should invariably be stopped in a manner that leads to a possible opening for a return (or counter) punch or punches. I might

Fig. 18.—Making an Opening by Breaking Opponent's Arms apart.

liken this to the good billiard player, who not only plays for the particular shot on the table, but for others to follow. His mind is always centred on the play to come, and he manipulates the balls accordingly. So it should be with the boxer. In either delivering or stopping a punch, he should have ulterior motives in his thoughts. Although an opponent may prevent these from materialising, their realisation will come sooner or later, for a conscientious boxer's maxim should always be : " Try, try again ! " Anyhow, in the case of the phase depicted in Fig. 14, the defensive object is but subservient to the offensive.

Having forced himself to close quarters, the in-fighter is here faced with the possible danger of a left to the face and right to the body. His object, as must always be the case, is naturally to administer punishment, the while he himself modifies the possibilities of receiving same.

Having slightly side-stepped the left, allowing it to brush past the ear, the in-fighter holds his opponent's right in check, the while he himself smashes his own right to the heart. In this case, both the defensive (or natural law) has succeeded, as well as the preconceived plan of attack.

Preconception in Boxing.

Unfortunately, preconception in boxing is very limited, for one never quite knows what an opponent will do. Billiard players may plan a dozen shots ahead, but the boxer is lucky if he can occasionally bring off such advantages as the one described in this chapter. There are moments, **ho**wever, when

Fig. 19—Using Left on the Opponent who Holds. (In my contest with Carpentier

an opponent is made to fall into certain trouble in spite of himself. That is where the more experienced boxer gets the better of another.

Reconnoitring when at Close Quarters.

Although having written in a previous chapter that it is rarely possible to use the eyes for "surveying" purposes while in close quarters, occasions do arise when this reconnoitring is of much advantage, that is, when presuming that the opportunity for so doing be given by an opponent.

Having proceeded into a lock-clinch, that is, when attack on either side seems hopeless, the moment is opportune for glancing at your man's jaw, the object being to see if it is in a position for a right jolt. If such be the case, then is the time to work the right gradually into a position for executing your project.

Care must be taken that your own right be well over your opponent's left, thus holding it in check. Otherwise, this peep from cover may prove costly.

Your man's right must also be held in such a manner as to prevent any action on its part.

If, when rushing to close quarters, the in-fighter's position is not as shown in Fig. 15, then he must so manœuvre his arms and legs as to bring it about. Once accomplished, he can risk the above-mentioned "survey" in the hope of finding the jaw exposed for attack. If this proves to be as hoped, then is the in-fighter's moment to strike, and strike quickly.

Placing the Right-Arm Jolt.

Having well worked his right to the inside of his man's left, and holding it in check as shown in

Fig. 20—Bringing about a Double Clinch for the Referee's Intervention
(An incident in my contest with Carpentier.)

Fig. 15, the possibility of receiving a left is thus prevented. It now remains for the in-fighter to push his opponent back by a jerk on his biceps, the brusque movement startling him. This ruse is necessary to momentarily trouble his mind as to the meaning of such a strange practice. As the said pushing is undertaken without precisely holding the biceps, there is little fear of the referee separating the combatants before the in-fighter has delivered his contemplated jolt-punch under the chin. As the effect of this blow is calculated to send the receiver's head back, thus disturbing his presence of mind, there should arise an opportunity to draw the left away from the opponent's right biceps and hook same to the body. This punch, however, is quite supplementary, and only possible if circumstances will allow, for the opponent will possibly catch hold of your left arm in an endeavour to save himself from reeling backward as the result of the objective punch, i.e., a jolt under the chin. This last-named is a most damaging blow if delivered with something of a lift from the shoulder, that is to say, it should carry the full force that would be employed in lifting a heavy dumb-bell.

The Jab.

It must not be confounded with the jab, which is but a rap to the face or body, carrying but trivial consequences. The expression "jabbing a man's head off," although often used by writers, is sometimes an inaccurate description of a series after series of half-arm left flicks. Although the process may be

Fig. 21—Hooking the Man who Holds.

called jabbing, the jab, in its relation to the punch, is difficult to define accurately. In any case it seems to me that decisive victories are seldom brought about by the aid of this mysterious "JAB." I have read reports of contests in which the critic referred to a boxer as "repeatedly stabbing an opponent with the left," etc. This stab must be some relation—a few times removed perhaps—to the jab. "Jab" appears to be the saving word of many an inexperienced youthful writer on boxing matters, which he applies to any or all doubtful punches. This must not be taken as a reflection on boxing writers proper, whom I have always found competent and just, but to the ambitious office-boy, who, while for the first time describing a contest, will bring in every word of the pugilistic vocabulary irrespective of its proper place. These are, happily, rare occurrences.

Beating an Opponent by Punching his Gloved Hands or Arms.

Although perhaps not strictly orthodox, the process of numbing an opponent's arms, by punching him thereon, is often a road to victory. As most people are acquainted with the crippling effects of a blow on the biceps, it is but necessary for me to recall the fact that it temporarily numbs the entire arm, rendering same at least momentarily helpless.

A deal of damage may be done in this manner, especially as the punches are delivered when the opponent least expects them.

The man who keeps his left forearm well over his stomach is an easy target for the arm-punch. There

Fig. 22—Hooking Right on finding the Left stopped by Moreau.

are several ways of administering this, i.e., either by driving your right on to your opponent's gloved fist, which at the time is protecting the " mark " (pit of the stomach), or by a smashing blow on his biceps.

In the first instance the impact of the punch, if delivered with force, should cause your opponent's own fist to sink into his stomach, thus perhaps " knocking himself out," so to speak. In any case, such a delivery can but be advantageous to the one who gets it well home, and distinctly uncomfortable for the other fellow. I have seen other boxers do this with varying effect. It is worth trying when opportunity calls.

Punching the Biceps.

The punch on the biceps is equally alarming to an opponent, for the result is sometimes of a no less painful nature than the above-mentioned stomach arm-punch.

The continual punching of a man's upper arm must, sooner or later, bring on a state of paralysis.

As the result of such maulings a boxer will often be forced to retire, actually believing that his arm is broken. A blow on what is known as the " funny bone "—which, by the way, is not a bone at all, but a nerve—produces much the same effect. But as the particular spot in that case is difficult to find, and the seeking for it may mean the wasting of many punches, the in-fighter should turn his attention to the biceps. The rule, therefore, is, that when no other part of an opponent's body is attackable go for his arms.

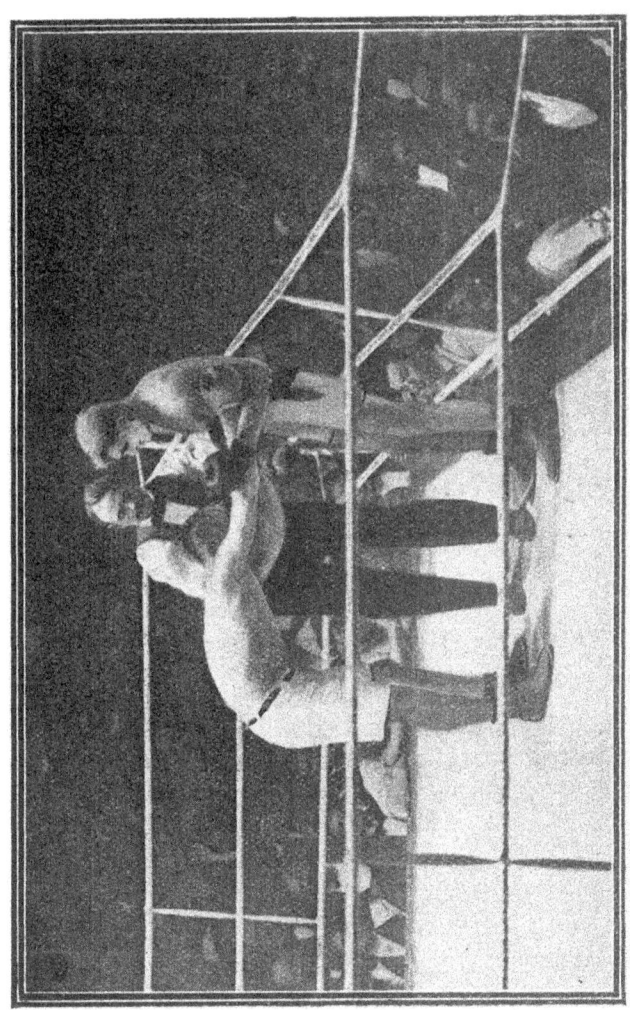

Fig. 23.—The safe "Break." (Photograph taken in my contest with Papke.)

Knocking a Man out by Punching his Gloved Fist.

I have knocked a man out who was covering his jaw by punching the gloved hand that was shielding that vulnerable point. Of course, my opponent was so unprepared for such an attack, and felt himself so secure, that he did not even attempt to counter the blow. He tried it on others later—with good results.

Many pugilistic prudes will no doubt look upon this arm-punching as rather sharp practice, many degrees removed from what these gentlemen would call the "clean style," but I maintain that a boxer's chief aim while in the ring is to beat his opponent. So long as he does this honestly, his manner of arriving at that desirable end surely concerns him alone.

Old-Fashioned Methods.

There are some people who abhor any but what are known as "old-fashioned" methods, but boxing, like all things, has gone ahead since those days, and the sooner young boxers realise this, the sooner will they secure world honours. I maintain that in-fighting is an all too-neglected art, one full of new interests, and not ugly to watch—when understood.

The art of self-defence surely implies the power and means to defend oneself at all times. How can a boxer do full credit to this doctrine and himself, if only partially armed for it?

In-fighting is a formidable adjunct to the integral art of boxing.

Fig. 24—The Left Arm in Chancery.

Breaking an Opponent's Arms apart to Facilitate an Attack.

This requires a deal of dexterity and quickness of eye, for in the event of missing the movement there is danger of taking a right or left to the jaw.

A good defensive out-fighter is often difficult to " get at." He will even creep up to the in-fighter, the while he keeps a protective guard, and hook a punch before the latter can stop it.

Having studied this particular tendency in an opponent, the thing is to find a means whereby he may be made to pay for his temerity.

Having allowed him to get near enough, it is necessary to suddenly penetrate inside his guard, and, as shown in the picture of Fig. 18, violently thrust his arms aside. If this be done sharply, and the movement executed with force, the shock will unbalance your opponent's mind and legs, causing an opening for a right half-arm upper-cut to the chin. This particular breaking apart of an opponent's arm is wonderfully efficacious, but the opportunities for its accomplishment are rare, although presenting themselves occasionally during a contest. I should not advise a boxer to attempt it until he has familiarised himself with the move, and feels himself capable of taking a chance now and then ; for in boxing, as in most things, one must often take risks to bring off big deals.

Some In-Fighting Phases taken from Actual Contests.

Being in possession of a few pictures of the various contests that I have engaged in during my stay in

Paris, I thought that these might prove interesting, depicting as they do various phases of the in-fighting art. As they represent actual facts, occurring during real combat, no better idea could be given of the efficacy of close-quarter boxing; for even while posing for the numerous photos in this book, there necessarily exists an artificial atmosphere of self-consciousness.

Punching the Opponent who Holds.

As will be seen in the accompanying picture of my contest with Georges Carpentier at Dieppe, the Frenchman has my right in chancery, thus preventing my using it either to the body or for hooking to the jaw.

In such an event, the in-fighter must at once draw his left arm well back from obstruction, and use same to the stomach. The referee is here seen stepping up to separate us, but as I had one arm free, and it was Carpentier who was holding me, no break should have been enforced until we were both holding. The rule of in-fighting is that a man may punch an opponent so long as the former has one or both hands available. In this instance my left arm was free, and although I cannot remember whether I was allowed to use it—which is doubtful seeing the referee's close proximity—I evidently was rightly about to do so. This reminds me that the in-fighter is a great deal at the mercy of the third man in a ring, for the breaking of two boxers, when their position does not exactly call for the order, is favouring (unwittingly perhaps) the long-range boxer. However, we have to take the good with the bad in boxing, and make the best of our time when close up, bringing in-fighting experience to bear detrimentally on an opponent.

When to Hold an Opponent and thus Call for the Break.

It occasionally happens during a contest that your opponent so holds as to negative any form of effective attack. Some boxers will pummel the back, shoulders, and other exposed but invulnerable parts, and in the process do themselves more harm than good. Every punch given by the in-fighter should have an object, and that object should be : the gradual or immediate beating of a man. Punches on the shoulder or back are so much waste of energy ; they are taken little notice of by the opponent, and still less by judges and referees. Therefore the better plan, in the event of being unable to land an efficient punch, is to bring about a clinch by also holding one's opponent, thus calling the break. As will be seen in this particular phase of my contest with Carpentier (Fig. 20) he is holding me in such a mnaner, with his head so low, as to leave but his back and kidneys exposed. As the latter must not be touched, this leaves the in-fighter but "Hobson's choice" of bringing about a speedy separation. In doing this I hugged the French champion in such a manner that he himself was so locked as to prevent him suddenly springing some surprise on me.

Hooking the Right while the Left is being Held.

The out-fighter's favourite trick is to hold one of his opponent's arms under his own, thus temporarily

Fig. 25—Punching Body with the Right, while Papke is Holding my Left.

silencing one gun, so to speak. In the course of my contest with Marcel Moreau at Aix-les-Bains, the latter frequently had recourse to this (see Fig. 21) mode of defence, which is invariably a sure sign that a man is not particularly keen on close-range exchanges. The boxer addicted to that practice will, in almost every case, simultaneously seek to get hold of your other arm. While the opponent is thus occupied it should be the in-fighter's plan to keep his free arm from being also put out of action, and, as in the present case, hook same to the jaw. The man who holds desperately is not inclined to mix matters at close quarters, his mind being far too occupied with defensive precautions.

Almost the same thing occurs in the phase shown in Fig. 22, except that Moreau has grasped my left arm, as it was making for his stomach, the while I am about to hook him with the right. Judging by his tactics, it was soon apparent to me that I had to deal with a boxer who did not relish in-fighting. My mind being thus fixed, I bored in all the more and won in four rounds.

Apart from that, I found Moreau to be one of the hardest-hitting boxers I have met in my career.

My Contest with Billy Papke.

Being an excellent in-fighter himself, I had more difficulty with Papke. The clashing of the identical styles means much that would not occur when opposed to a man possessed of but the out-fighting art. Papke is equally clever at both styles, and this fact made my battle with him all the more bitter and interesting. Although we both tried to

Fig. 26—A Peculiar Incident : Papke Falling on to a Punch.

knock each other out in a reckless first round, I found that it was more prudent to out-general him in in-fighting, and gradually reduce him to nought. This I accomplished successfully, mostly by continued and direct attacks to his body, occasionally varied by some long-range straight lefts and right swings to the jaw.

As I said in the beginning of this book, my plan was to force him as often as possible to the ropes (see Fig. 23) and while there worry him, thereby affecting his morale. I soon realised that he was gradually giving way under the force of these onslaughts, so repeated them as often as possible. In the picture the referee has just ordered the " break," and it will be noticed that I am carrying out the order in the safest manner possible, as hereafter described.

Breaking away Safely.

Many a man has been beaten through sheer carelessness while breaking away from a clinch after close-work fighting. A boxer should always live up to the belief that so long as an opponent is in the ring he is dangerous ; but in few cases is this fact more potential than when breaking away. So long as both men are free either can punch, and a quick-footed opponent may smash a blow home before you have had time to regain your protective guard.

It is therefore advisable to keep a sharp eye on an adversary's eyes and arms when leaving a clinch, at the same time working your own so that he cannot possibly catch you " on the hop," so to speak. The experienced in-fighter will, therefore, get well inside

Fig. 27—George Engel, Manager to Frank Klaus.

his opponent's arms and hold same in check in the manner shown in the illustration. The man thus placed can neither use his right nor left with any degree of success, if at all. There is a great deal in this, for having finally stepped clear, it gives one time to regain one's natural guard, or at once rush the opponent, according to the situation created by the said break. Action must then rest on the existing possibilities, for if the opponent has also assumed a safe guard the in-fighter must be guided by his next move.

Holding an Arm in Chancery.

As was the case with Marcel Moreau (see Fig. 21), Billy Papke frequently lent himself to the chancery trick, thereby checking my left arm. In Fig. 24 Papke is seen holding, just after having tried to hook his left to the jaw. By sending my head down on his shoulder, the punch landed on the neck. This movement allowed me not only to see that the body was exposed to a punch with my right, but facilitated my getting it there. It must have been a pretty hard one, too, for Papke's legs gave the signal of distress mentioned elsewhere. Almost the same thing occurs in the following picture, Papke holding my left arm in submission while I used my right on his body.

Falling on to a Stomach Punch.

This was a rarer phase of my contest with Papke, one which occurs but seldom. The in-fighter must however, be awake for all emergencies and have the necessary remedy handy. In trying a terrific right swing, which he missed, owing to my having ducked same, Papke fell clean on to a right punch to the stomach, supplemented by a left to the liver. As this happened toward the end of the bout, when my opponent was already well on the road to defeat, it must have proved pretty disastrous. But all this does not alter the fact that I took a good many hard punches myself during those fourteen and a quarter rounds; they, however, meant my securing the middle-weight championship of the world.

Training.

As a boxer's training methods seem to interest most people, I should like to say a few words on that particular subject.

Apart from as much practice as possible in the gymnasium in the hope of either perfecting already acquired knowledge, and gleaning more, a boxer's training should depend a great deal upon his own temperament. Apart from the stereotyped, irksome, but necessary methods of taking off weight, I think that some boxers work too hard. A good trainer should at once be able to gauge his man's working capacity, and not unduly tax same. Plenty of open-air roadwork amid rural and health-giving surroundings is the principal item, with plenty of wholesome non-fat-producing foods.

I would also recommend the Muller* system of exercises as distinctly healthful, and invaluable for keeping fit when not in active training, and particularly for strengthening the muscles of the abdomen

* See Advertisement on page 75.

and improving the wind. " Gym " work must be regulated according to one's requirements. For example, if one's wind be not quite sound, then skipping should be prolonged. As all the other phases of a boxer's training are familiar, it but remains for me to thank all those who have given me their sympathy and support during my long tramp up the road that leads to pugilistic success, and to crave the indulgence of my readers for the shortcomings of this little book.

My great hope is, that it may be the means of doing as much good to those who study it as it has to me by long practising of all its various points.

A Selection Of Classic Instructive Titles Relating To The Art Of Pugilism & Self Defence In Both War & Peace
Find our entire selection @ naval-military-press.com

ALL-IN FIGHTING
The distilled knowledge of W.E. Fairbairn, legendary SOE instructor in unarmed combat, and inventor of the Sykes-Fairbairn knife, who learned his deadly skills in 30 years on the Shanghai waterfront. Fully illustrated.
9781847348531

ART OF BOXING AND SCIENCE OF SELF DEFENCE
Former Lightweight Champion Billy Edwards shares the techniques and strategies of the sweet science in his beautifully illustrated boxing guide. Explore boxing's transition from bare knuckle spectacle to today's Marquis of Queensbury ruleset.
9781474539548

SELF DEFENCE OR THE ART OF BOXING

Ned Donnelly was a pioneer of boxing training during the late Victorian era. Explore the strategies and techniques used by this trainer of champions via a series of easy-to-follow illustrations and clear, concise coaching steps.

9781474539562

JACK GOODWIN'S BOXING

This 1920's boxing masterpiece by Jack Goodwin puts you in the shoes of a coach in that era. Uncover the best ways to run, manage and train boxers as taught by Jack Goodwin, a champion and trainer of champions in the noble science.

9781474539586

THE COMPLETE BOXER

Gunner Moir provides detailed instructions on the techniques he deployed to become British Heavyweight Champion. Taught in a series of easy to learn techniques, combinations, and boxing strategies.

9781474539609

ART OF WRESTLING

George de Relwyskow Army Gymnastic Staff

In the appreciation to this book Captain Daniels, V.C., M.C., Rifle Brigade, states: "In adding a word to this book on the style of wrestling as taught at the Headquarters Gymnasium of the British Army, and having had personal experience in the various holds and throws taught, I consider it has been of great value in the training of the soldier, and the bringing out of those qualities of grit and determination which have been seen in all ranks who have taken an active part throughout the greatest war in history." 1919.

9781783313563

KILL OR GET KILLED

Rex Applegate's "kill or be killed" helped prepare America's marines, soldiers, sailors, spies and airmen for the realities of war. This highly shared and respected work provides all you need to know about unarmed combat and close quarter engagement with the enemy.

9781474539661

BOXING (V-Five)
The Aviation Training Office of the Chief of Naval Operations

The game-changing V-Five suite of training manuals helped get a generation of American aviators fit for war. Here we explore how the airmen of the US navy trained in boxing as part of their military fitness regime.

9781474539623

THE TEXTBOOK OF WRESTLING

Get your wrestling skills matt-ready from wrestling champion and world-renown trainer Ernest Gruhn. Replete with detailed holds, throws, pins and strategies for success in a wide range of wrestling rulesets.

9781474539647

MANUAL OF PHYSICAL TRAINING 1914
(United States Army)

Published just prior to the outbreak of World War 1, this beautifully illustrated guide was designed to revolutionise the combat fitness and readiness of the US Army covering a wide range of gymnastic and combat calisthenic exercises.

9781474539708

DEAL THE FIRST DEADLY BLOW
United States Department of the Army

This Vietnam-era classic showcases in detail how the US Forces trained in close quarter combat. Known as the "encyclopaedia of combat" it helped a generation learn how to become devastating effective with empty hands, knives and bayonets alike.

9781474539722

HAND-TO-HAND COMBAT
Bureau of Aeronautics U.S Navy 1943

This is one of the best combative manuals from World War 2, developed by the US Navy V-Five Staff, that included the renowned American wrestler Wesley Brown. It is then not especially surprising that wrestling skills predominate in this manual, and form the base skill-set for this combative system.

9781474537391

ABWEHR ENGLISCHER GANGSTER METHODEN DEFENSE OF ENGLISH GANGSTERS METHODS – SILENT KILLING – FULL ENGLISH TRANSLATION

In 1942 the Wehrmacht published a training manual with the goal of countering the "silent killing" tactics used by the British commando units. The manual was – much in line with typical National Socialist terminology –titled

"Abwehr Englischer Gangster-methoden" or "Defence Against English Gangster methods".

This book was compiled due the Wehrmacht intelligence operatives uncovering of a British hand-to-hand course for the SOE, Commandos, et al, on methods of quick and silent killing (undoubtedly developed by W. E. Fairbairn and E. A. Sykes). They correctly assessed that their troops in general and particularly the Geheime Staatspolizei (Gestapo), Sicherheitsdienst (SD), their security guards, and sentries would be in grave danger when confronted by men trained in these methods. This manual/program was the Wehrmacht's response.

9781474538336

BOXING FOR BOYS

Regtl. Sergt.-Major E B Dent Army Gymnastic Headquarters

A successful system of boxing instruction for large classes, to allow tuition with no detriment to the "backward or shy pupil". Covers Kit-On, Guard-Sparring-Advance-Point & Mark-Ducking-Medicine, Bag-Left & Right Hooks etc. The author considered that boxing systematically taught to the youth was beneficial exercise, and would have a marked elevating influence on the national character.

9781783314607

HAND-TO-HAND FIGHTING

A System Of Personal Defence For The Soldier (1918)

A tough book on the art of hand to hand fighting in the trenches of the Great War. Demonstrating techniques utilised to "do away with the enemy", many of which are barred in clean wrestling, the book includes good clear photographic illustrations presenting important attack methods including the "Hammer Lock", "Kidney Kick", "Head Twist", "Knee Groin Kick", and the "Knee Break", all very important in a man to man, life or death encounter, when fighting in the mud of the trenches.

9781783313983

HAND TO HAND COMBAT

Francois d'Eliscu taught thousands of U.S. Army Rangers how to fight down and dirty in World War II. d'Eliscu doesn't get the press that Fairbairn and Applegate do, but he did a commendable job writing this book. It is basic, meant for training raw recruits in a short amount of time before sending them to the front, but simple is good when you are in combat, as most combative experts' will tell you.

9781474535823

COLD STEEL

A cold-war combatives classic. John Styers, US Marine and WW2 veteran, lays out his approach to close quarters combat with rifle, bayonet, stick, knife and empty hands. Explore what helped wartime and post-war Marines stay ahead of the competition with lucid imagery and clear combative descriptions.

9781474540643

THE COMPLETE KANO JIU-JITSU

Join world-famous physical culture expert H. Irving Hancock, and Jiu-Jitsu specialist Katsukama Higashi as they showcase the art of 'Kano Jiu-Jitsu' now known as Judo. Get an exclusive glimpse into the transitional era of the martial art, alongside how it uses Japanese physical culture methodologies for self-improvement.

9781474540735

WE Fairbairn's Complete Compendium of Lethal, Unarmed, Hand-to-Hand Combat Methods and Fighting In Colour

All 844 images of Fairbairn and his assistants can now for the first time be seen in full colour, lending a clarity to the practical methods of mastering the manner of dealing with an assailant, both in time of war and when placed in difficulty during unpleasant modern urban situations. These various holds, trips, kicks, blows etc, allow the average man or woman a position of security against almost any form of armed or unarmed attack. Captain W.E. Fairbairn would have approved of this new colour version, that gives an illustrative clarity to the original that was lacking in previous monochrome reprints of his work.

All six of W.E. Fairbairn's works in one binding to create the ultimate colour compendium: Get Tough-All-In Fighting-Shooting to Live-Scientific Self-Defence-Hands Off!-Defend

9781783318735

SELF DEFENCE FOR WOMEN COMBATO

Join the Canadian combatives legend William "Bill" Underwood as he showcases self-defence for women. Over the course of clear photography, sketches and instructions he lays out a curriculum for self-defence for the attacks women would be most likely to face.

9781474540711

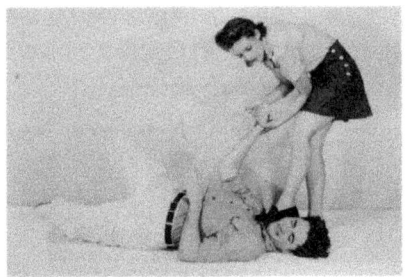

SCIENTIFIC UNARMED COMBAT
The Art of Dynamic Self-Defence

Learn the esoteric Sri Lankan art of 'Cheena-Adi' with R. A Vairamuttu. This guide explores armed and unarmed self-defence drawing heavily from Indian martial culture, alongside wellness and development from Indian physical culture, fitness, diet and medicine.

9781474540728

THE NEW SCIENCE
Weaponless Defence

Join wrestling champions Prof F. S Lewis, William V Gregory and Boxing Champ Tommy Burns as they showcase street orientated self-defence from people with a proven track record of fighting success. This 1906 manual via a series of photos and instructions lays out simple, tried and tested ways to keep yourself safe.

9781474540704

COMBAT CONDITIONING MANUAL
Jiu-Jitsu Defence, Bayonet Defence and Club Defence

This 1942 guide for marines lays out the basics of combat Ju Jitsu as part of an overall training regimen for US Marines. It's a holistic guide that covers defences against armed and unarmed attackers, physical fitness and even first aid.

9781474540698

BOXING TAUGHT THROUGH "SLOW MOTION FILM"

Learn the ropes from the best fighters of the 1900s-1930s in this unique boxing manual. Using stills from super slow-mo fight footage, this treasure trove unpacks the skills, tips and tactics of the champs for you to emulate at home.

9781474540681

HOW TO BOX CORRECTLY

Explore the art of boxing according to famous Bronx boxing brand Ben Lee in this 1944 how-to guide. Learn the ropes from one of the nation's top trainers and boxing journalists John J. Romano, in this warmly illustrated guide to the sweet science.

9781474540674

THE ART OF IN-FIGHTING BY FRANK KLAUS

German-American Middleweight Champ Frank Klaus showcases his KO-scoring boxing IQ in this 1913 guide. Containing clear and easy to understand photography and descriptions, Klaus gives us an insight into the emerging hard-hitting American style of professional boxing.

9781474541473

THE ART OF BOXING AND HINTS ON TRAINING

Crafted just after WW1 in 1919, this guide by Royal Naval Physical Training, Chief Staff Instructor J.O'Neil explores the military benefits of boxing. Showcasing via lucid text and full page photography.

9781474541510

JIM DRISCOLL'S TEXTBOOK OF BOXING

Driscoll was a former Featherweight World Champion and in this 1914 guide, he uses cutting edge and clear photography to showcase the new scientific boxing method. Driscoll showcases to the audience the way to best combine British and American boxing training and fighting philosophy.

9781474541466

JUDO AND ITS USE IN HAND TO HAND COMBAT FROM SEABEES NAVAL ENGINEERING CORPS

Brought to you by William Caldwell of the Seabees Naval Engineering Corps. This WW2 close combat classic provides an insight into the "Combat Judo" used by the navy to prepare personnel for the dangers of theatre. Fully photographed and accessible with clear instructional content to follow.

9781474541480

HAND TO HAND COMBAT - Field Manual 21-150

An example of Cold War / Korean War close combat training. Filled with instructor notes and clear imagery covering unarmed and "cold weapon" combat such as bayonet, knife and garrotte.

9781474541459

AMERICAN JUDO ILLUSTRATED
Brought to you by William Caldwell of the Seabees Naval Engineering Corps. This WW2 close combat classic provides an insight into the "Combat Judo" used by the navy to prepare personnel for the dangers of theatre. Fully photographed and accessible with clear instructional content to follow.
9781474541527

BOXING
This 1906 guide from former English Heavyweight Champion Captain Johnstone, showcases the leading techniques, skills, strategies and fighting philosophies of the day. Brought to life with vivid storytelling from military boxing advocates alongside lucid photography and crisp follow-along guidance for boxers to follow.
9781474541534

KILL OR GET KILLED
Lt Col. Rex Applegate's WW2 Combat Classic 'Kill or Get Killed' is one of the most detailed and comprehensive guides of armed and unarmed combat ever written. From unarmed, to knife, bayonet, pistol, garotte and more – Applegate provides written descriptions, photographs, illustrations on more to showcase and share the skills of forces like the O.S.S.
9781474541541

BALL PUNCHING - A PICTORIAL GUIDE TO THE SPEEDBAG
This 1922 guide from Tom Carpenter is a response to the 'speedbag' craze of the early part of the century. It showcases via clear instructions and photography how to best use tools such as maize, speed and double-end bags for fitness and fighting skills.
9781474541503

SCIENTIFIC BOXING FROM A FISTIC EXPERT
Diet - Fight Training - K.O. Punching
This 1937 guide to the American school and style of professional boxing provides a clear and well-illustrated suite of technical skills and drills to compete successfully. Replete with training advice, rule guidance and ring Generalship principles to help boxers be inline with the latest advice and training acumen.
9781474541497

www.ingramcontent.com/pod-product-compliance
Lightning Source LLC
LaVergne TN
LVHW010319070426
835510LV00031B/3453